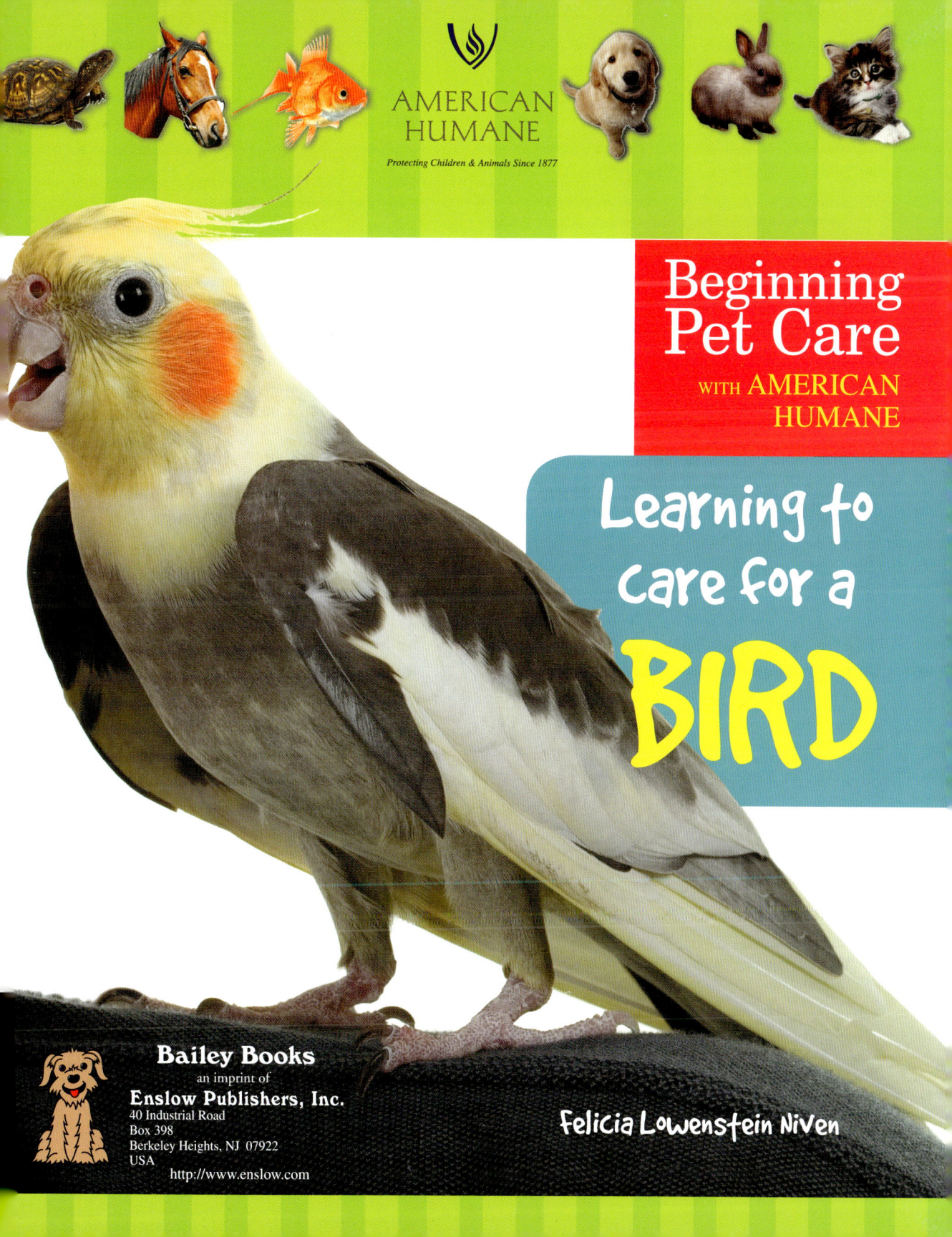

AMERICAN HUMANE
Protecting Children & Animals Since 1877

Beginning Pet Care
WITH AMERICAN HUMANE

Learning to Care for a BIRD

Bailey Books
an imprint of
Enslow Publishers, Inc.
40 Industrial Road
Box 398
Berkeley Heights, NJ 07922
USA
http://www.enslow.com

Felicia Lowenstein Niven

AMERICAN HUMANE
Protecting Children & Animals Since 1877

Founded in 1877, the American Humane Association is the only national organization dedicated to protecting both children and animals. Through a network of child and animal protection agencies and individuals, American Humane develops policies, legislation, curricula, and training programs — and takes action — to protect children and animals from abuse, neglect, and exploitation. To learn how you can support American Humane's vision of a nation where no child or animal will ever be a victim of abuse or neglect, visit www.americanhumane.org, phone (303) 792-9900, or write to the American Humane Association at 63 Inverness Drive East, Englewood, Colorado, 80112-5117.

To our Readers:
We have done our best to make sure all Internet Addresses in this book were active and appropriate when we went to press. However, the author and the publisher have no control over and assume no liability for the material available on those Internet sites or on other Web sites they may link to. Any comments or suggestions can be sent by e-mail to comments@enslow.com or to the address on the back cover.

Every effort has been made to locate all copyright holders of material used in this book. If any errors or omissions have occurred, corrections will be made in future editions of this book.

Bailey Books, an imprint of Enslow Publishers, Inc.

Copyright © 2011 by Enslow Publishers, Inc.

All rights reserved.

No part of this book may be reproduced by any means without the written permission of the publisher.

Library of Congress Cataloging-in-Publication Data

Niven, Felicia Lowenstein.
  Learning to care for a bird / Felicia Lowenstein Niven.
    p. cm.—(Beginning pet care with American Humane)
  Includes bibliographical references and index.
  Summary: "Readers will learn how to choose, train, and care for a bird"—Provided by publisher.
  ISBN 978-0-7660-3192-0
  1. Cage birds—Juvenile literature. I. Title.
SF461.35.N58 2010
636.6'8—dc22
                                    2008048964

Printed in China

052010 Leo Paper Group, Heshan City, Guangdong, China

10 9 8 7 6 5 4 3 2 1

Illustration Credits: All animals in the logo bar and boxes, Shutterstock. © Buena Vista Pictures/courtesy Everett Collection, pp. 40-41; Carolyn A. McKeone, courtesy of Exotic Wings Canada, K. Davey/Photo Researchers, Inc., pp. 3 (thumbnail 3), 16; Carolyn A. McKeone/Photo Researchers, Inc., pp. 20, 26, 42; Christine Osborne/Photo Researchers, Inc., pp. 3 (thumbnail 2), 9; HIRB/photolibrary, p. 18; Image100 Limited/photolibrary, p. 25; © istockphoto.com/Jill Lang, pp. 7, 31; © istockphoto.com/Robert Byron, pp. 36-37; © istockphoto.com/Serdar Yagci, pp. 3 (thumbnail 5), 33; Picture Partners/Photolibrary, pp. 3 (thumbnail 6), 43; Shutterstock, pp. 1, 3 (thumbnails 1, 4), 4-5, 11, 12, 13, 15, 21, 24, 27, 29, 34, 35, 44; © Tony Freeman/PhotoEdit, p. 23.

Cover Illustration: Shutterstock (cockatiel).

1 Rescue.................... 4

2 History of the Bird........... 9

3 Getting a Bird.............. 13

4 Health and Exercise.......... 21

5 Problems and Challenges 29

6 A Lifelong Responsibility...... 40

   Glossary 45

   Further Reading............. 46
   (Books and Internet Addresses)

   Index..................... 48

Chapter 1
Rescue

Brando was a beautiful bird. He was the type of parrot that you might see on travel brochures. He had lots of colorful feathers and a twinkle in his eyes.

But he did not speak. That was unusual. His species of parrot, the macaw, is often a good talker. It was a mystery. The couple that adopted him did not know why he did not speak. They loved him anyway, even though Brando could only whistle and squawk.

Brando was a macaw like this one.

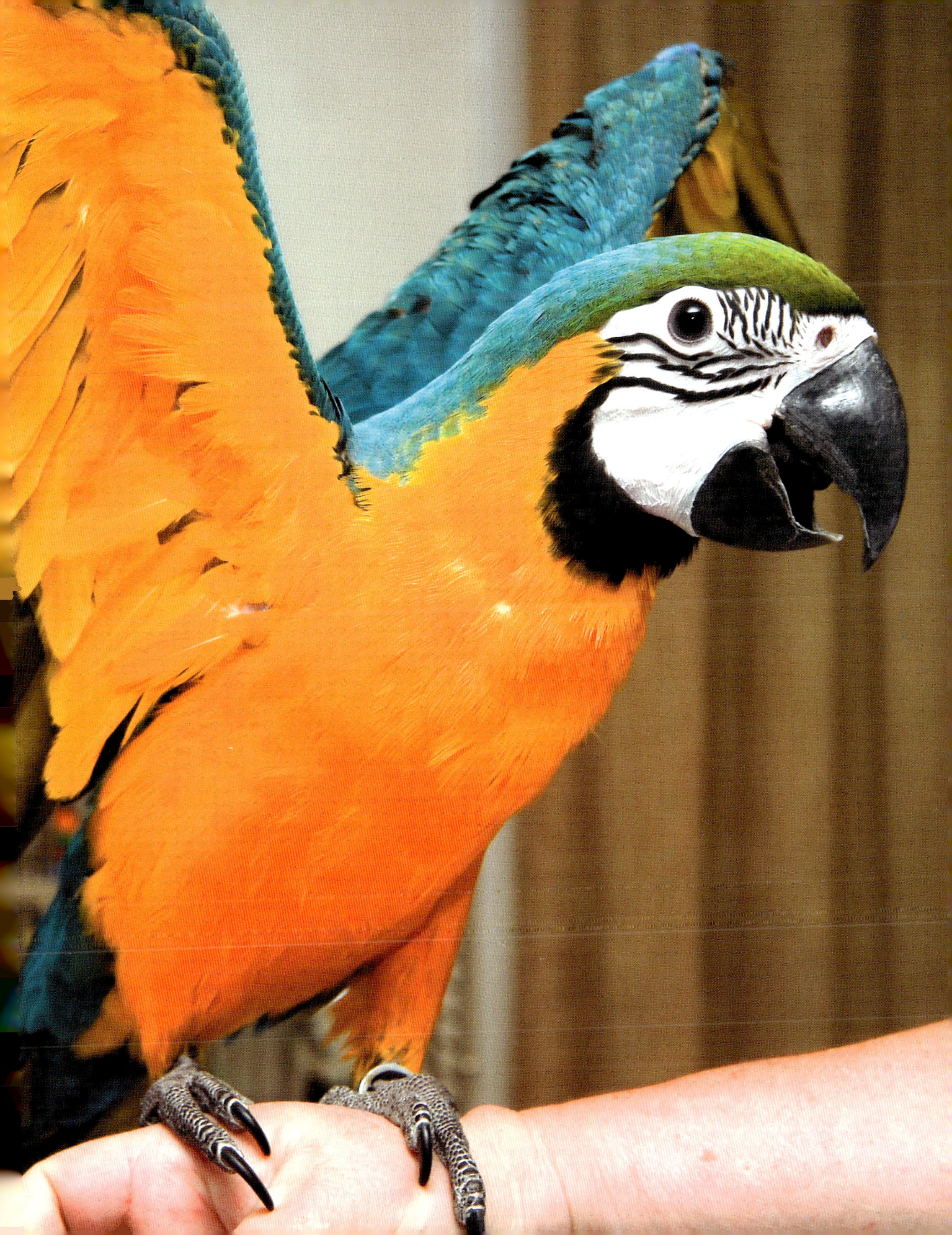

Rescue

Then, it happened. Without any warning one night, Brando spoke.

"Help me! Please, someone help me!"

The couple was confused. Did Brando want to be rescued from them? Maybe he was just repeating something he heard? Did they leave the TV on? Did one of them say that phrase recently?

They stayed perfectly quiet, waiting for Brando to speak again.

"Help me! Please, won't someone help me?" The parrot's voice was loud and clear.

The couple opened the window and listened. There was the sound of traffic. But maybe, just maybe, there was a faint voice calling for help. The wife phoned 911. The husband went outside with a flashlight.

It was hard to tell if there was a voice. The car horns were loud. There was a lot of traffic. The husband walked across the street. There was

Rescue

nothing there but some old warehouses. Still, he thought he heard something.

"I'm over here! Please help me!"

The old man was pinned between a van and the warehouse wall. His name was Edward Kabrick. He used to be a plumber. At age seventy, he still did a little work. He had gone to his warehouse to get some supplies. Somehow, his van had rolled down the hill. So Kabrick was stuck between the van and the wall, unable to move.

Macaws are very smart birds!

Rescue

He had broken his ribs and his legs. He was in terrible pain. He had been calling out for help for hours.

The police arrived just at that moment. They rescued Kabrick.

"I thought I would surely freeze to death if no one found me soon," Kabrick said as he was put into an ambulance. "Thank you for hearing my cries for help. I didn't think I would be able to last the night."

The couple explained that they had not heard his cries. Brando had.

The policeman shook his head. "You found Mr. Kabrick because your parrot repeated his cries for help? I would call that some kind of miracle."

"Yes," the husband told the officer. "I think that 'miracle' will be the next word we'll teach him."

Excerpted, edited, and reprinted with permission from Animal Miracles by Brad Steiger and Sherry Hansen Steiger.

Chapter 2
History of the Bird

Ancient Egyptians kept birds as pets. This art shows the Egyptian god Horus as a bird.

About four thousand years ago, people in Egypt did something unusual for that time. They put birds in cages. Others before them saw birds as food. The Egyptians did not. They saw something beautiful in the doves and parrots that they kept. These were the first pet birds.

History of the Bird

The Egyptians kept some birds in the pharaoh's royal zoo. They painted pictures of them. That is how we know about these early pets.

Birds turned out to be very good pets. They whistled and sang. They copied noises. Some could even talk. They were also very useful.

Pigeons could carry messages. They could be trained to return again and again to a certain spot. The Greeks and Romans used them to send messages home when they were fighting battles.

A famous Greek named Aristotle had a pet parrot. He used to write about him. In fact, the scientific name for the parrot family Psittacidae (sit-UH-suh-dee) comes from the name that Aristotle called his bird Psittace.

Alexander the Great also had a pet bird. His was a parakeet. It was a gift from one of his generals, after his army conquered India.

History of the Bird

When Christopher Columbus discovered the New World, he brought back a pair of Cuban Amazon parrots. They were a gift to Queen Isabella. This was not the first time a bird lived in a palace. Pet birds lived in many royal households. Their job was to entertain their owners.

Around the same time, one tiny kind of bird had a special job. The canary went down into mine shafts with miners. His job was to save the miners' lives. Sometimes there were poisonous gases in the mines. The canary was very tiny. The gas affected the bird much quicker than a person. So if the canary got sleepy, that was the signal to get out quickly.

This is a canary.

History of the Bird

Canaries are not used for this job anymore. But pigeons are still used to carry messages sometimes. And all birds continue to provide enjoyment to their owners, even if they are not royalty.

Over the years, people began breeding birds for certain traits. Perhaps they wanted more colorful feathers. Maybe they wanted a certain sound. This led to many popular types of pet birds.

Today there are about ten thousand different kinds of birds. They are as small as the hummingbird or as large as the ostrich. Today, as in ancient Egypt, birds bring us great joy and can make wonderful pets.

This is a hummingbird.

Chapter 3
Getting a Bird

Lady Gouldian Finches are just one type of colorful bird.

If you are thinking about getting a feathered friend, you are not alone. There are 35 million to 45 million pet birds in the United States. That is because birds make great pets.

Getting a Bird

There are reasons why birds make great pets. Some birds, such as parrots, are smart. They like to be with people. They are nice looking and do not require a lot of grooming. In fact, they are quite easy to care for and not that expensive to feed. They also live a long time.

It is important, however, to get the right bird for your family. This will make the difference between a happy pet experience and a miserable one.

Birds come in many colors and sizes. You will find them in bright reds, yellows, greens, and blues. They also come in dull grays and browns. Finches measure about four inches from the tip of their beak to their tail. Compare that to a parrot whose wings stretch more than three feet across!

You cannot choose just on size and looks, though. Each species has a different temperament, or personality. Some birds are loud. Others are quieter. Some like to be handled. Others prefer to be left alone.

Getting a Bird

Some birds need a lot of attention. Large parrots and cockatoos are like this. These birds need daily time with their owners. Canaries and finches, on the other hand, prefer the company of their own kind to that of people.

This is a cockatoo.

Certain types of birds bond to just one person for life. The bird will follow that one person everywhere. She may be upset if he is not around. This might be a problem for a family pet.

You must also take into account the amount of space you have. Large parrots require a large cage. If you live in an apartment, look for a smaller bird. If you have neighbors close by, a quiet bird is a better fit too.

Getting a Bird

If you have a larger space, you may want to get more than one bird. That also depends on the species you choose.

Some birds, such as finches, need to be with others of their own kind. They will not do well if kept by themselves. However, others, such as macaws and cockatoos, are more easily trained and form a stronger bond with their owner if kept alone.

Getting a Bird

Also, just because the birds are the same species does not guarantee they will get along.

Your local library is a good place to learn about the many species of birds. The Internet is also a good place to learn about birds, but be sure to ask a trusted adult to help you search. The general rule is that the bigger the bird, the louder, messier, and more demanding he will be. Once you narrow down your choices, you can learn even more at a local bird club.

There are several places to get a bird. Your local animal shelter or bird rescue group is a good place to start. Also, members of a bird club can recommend breeders who take good care of the birds they raise and sell.

Take the time to make sure the bird is healthy. She should come from a clean place. There should be a roomy cage and lots of water. Your bird should have bright, clear eyes. She should be active.

Before you bring your bird home, make sure it is healthy.

Getting a Bird

Beware of birds that huddle or have droopy or missing feathers. Avoid birds with stains around the eyes. These are signs that the bird is not healthy.

Your new bird may be young or old. Either way, your bird should be able to eat on his own. Very young birds that are away from their parents must be hand-fed. That is the job of the breeder or pet store. Do not get a bird that must be hand-fed unless you know a lot about it. Otherwise, there could be problems.

Make sure that you get your new bird checked by a veterinarian. Choose a vet who has experience with birds. Some vets are specially trained in avian, or bird, medicine.

On the first visit, the vet will check your bird. He or she will take a sample of blood. This will help the vet check for early signs of disease.

Best of all, the vet can answer your questions. Write them down so you do not forget what you want to know.

Bird Examination Chart

Chapter 4
Health and Exercise

Your new bird will need a cage.

Before you bring your new bird home, you will need some supplies.

You will need a bird cage. A cage is where your bird lives. It keeps her safe.

Make sure the cage is big enough for your bird. She should be able to move around easily. For larger birds, cages should be at least one-and-a-half times as wide as their wingspan. If you have more than one bird, the cage should be even bigger.

Health and Exercise

Where you put the cage is just as important. Some birds are social. They need to be in the center of family life. Other birds need a quieter place.

Kitchens are not usually good places for birds. You also would not put a cage in direct sunlight or in front of an air conditioner or drafty window or door. The cage should be in a place that is not too warm or too cold.

Since birds do not sweat, you need to watch for signs that your bird is too hot. They may hold out their wings to cool down. They may also take baths. If they pant, they may be overheated.

If it is too cold, birds will sit on their feet. They will fluff up their feathers. Fluffed feathers may also mean they are ill. A comfortable temperature will help keep your bird healthy.

In addition to a cage, you will need food for your bird. Birds eat a mix of seeds, grains, vegetables, and fruits. You can buy bird food at the pet store,

Health and Exercise

supermarket, or vet's office. There are even special food mixes for certain species.

Fresh water is important each day. You can use a water bottle as long as your bird knows how to drink from it.

You will not need a lot of grooming tools. Birds use their beaks to clean their feathers. You just need clippers to trim their claws.

Your bird needs fresh food and water every day.

Health and Exercise

Check with your vet to make sure you're feeding your bird the right kind of bird seed.

An adult should trim their claws. But you do not want to trim them too much. Otherwise, your bird could lose his balance on a perch. Many bird owners clip just the needle-like tip of the claw. That way they do not get scratched.

Some owners have their bird's wing feathers clipped by a vet. This way the bird cannot fly. It does not hurt the bird. It prevents him from accidentally flying away through an open door or window.

Those feathers will grow back. You will need to have them clipped by a vet after every molt, or about once per year.

Even if they cannot fly away, birds do need to exercise, just like people. A cage with perches and toys will help make that happen.

Some birds need to be let out of their cages for exercise. Make sure you watch your bird very carefully.

Health and Exercise

You can also let your bird out of the cage. Many birds enjoy this freedom. It exercises their mind as well as their body. Just be watchful. There are many dangers for pet birds when they are out of the cage.

It is also a good idea to identify your bird. One way is by putting a band around his leg. Your vet can do this. Another method is the microchip. This is a small computer chip that is put into your bird's chest by a vet. The vet does this by first giving the bird medicine so it will not be painful. Sometimes vets put birds under anesthesia to do this.

Your bird may like toys in its cage.

Health and Exercise

Your bird should visit the vet for a wellness checkup about once a year. You can schedule a visit if your bird looks ill. Just keep in mind that birds often pretend they are not sick when they are. This dates back to their time in the wild. If another animal knew a bird was sick, he might attack. So look for small changes in your bird. For example, a chatty bird that becomes quieter might be feeling ill.

Finally, some animals are spayed or neutered. Spaying and neutering are operations that prevent animals from having babies. It is called spaying for a female and neutering for a male. Birds are not usually spayed or neutered. Therefore, you will want to keep male birds and female birds apart, so they do not have baby birds.

Chapter 5
Problems and Challenges

This is an African Grey parrot playing with a special bird toy.

Problems and Challenges

Each morning, in her Egg Harbor Township, New Jersey, home, Doreen Kohr has her coffee. You might say her African Grey parrot, Bo, has hers too. But Bo does not actually drink. She just makes the sounds of sipping coffee and putting the cup down. She also makes the sound of the squeaky door whenever visitors arrive or leave.

"I fixed that door ages ago, but it will always squeak because of Bo," said Kohr.

Birds like to mimic sounds. Some birds do it more easily than others. Some birds are able to copy human speech.

You can encourage a bird to make certain sounds or speak a word. Repeat the word or sound often in front of the bird. Reward him with a treat whenever he gets close. Once your bird learns one word or sound, he will learn new words and sounds more quickly.

It is also important to socialize your bird. That means getting him used to people.

Some parrots may be able to learn to speak a word or will make certain sounds. Try it and be patient!

Problems and Challenges

The McNeill family takes their Caique parrot, Zeke, to soccer games. He sits on the shoulders of thirteen-year-old Natalie or eight-year-old Isabel on bike rides.

"We take him wherever we can, even if it's just a trip to the hardware store," said Susan McNeill. She and husband Don recently had Zeke out with the girls at the local ice cream shop. "He's very affectionate. Zeke is an unbelievable bird and perfect for a family with kids."

Taking a bird like Zeke out of his cage helps him learn about the world. It keeps life from getting boring. But you need to be careful. The world can be a dangerous place.

Make sure your bird is safe and stays near you. Some larger birds will wear a harness once they get used to it. Never leave your bird alone in a car with the windows closed. On a warm day, it can get hot very quickly. If your bird is outside, be aware of other animals. They can frighten, or even attack, your bird.

An expert at a pet store or your vet will be able to help you if your bird is showing aggression. This person gently pets a macaw.

    Your house has dangers too. Common items, from suntan lotion to nail polish, are poisonous to birds. So are some houseplants, crayons, certain cleaners, and perfume. Birds have been caught in blankets and accidentally thrown into the clothes dryer. They have been stuck in toilets. They have even

Problems and Challenges

flown into closed windows and mirrors because they did not understand what they were. The list is very long. The best thing to do is to watch your bird whenever she is out of her cage.

Household hazards are one challenge. Sometimes you might also have problems with your bird's behavior. Here are some common ones.

Pecking/Aggression

Birds do not have teeth. But they do have sharp beaks. Sometimes they use them to peck people. Birds peck for different reasons. They may be scared or hurt. Baby birds may be pecking playfully.

These are two baby macaws. They are about six weeks old.

Problems and Challenges

Birds may also peck during mating season. They sometimes do it to show they are in control.

Try to find the cause behind the peck. Then work to get your bird comfortable so it stops. You can use treats when you handle your bird. If you cannot touch your bird without her pecking, wear oven mitts. Keep your voice calm and soft. Take time each day to hold your bird. Show her that it is safe and fun to be together.

If your bird does peck, say "no" firmly. Put her right back into her cage. Do not yell at her. Some birds like noise. They may repeat the behavior because of it.

Believe it or not — crayons are dangerous to your pet bird! Be sure to put them away if you take your pet out of his cage.

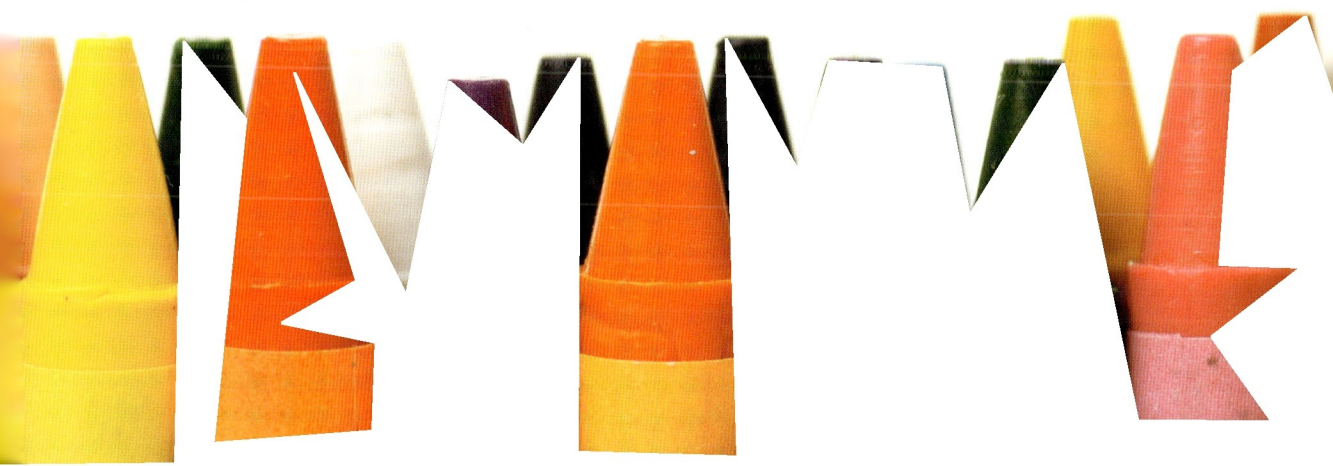

Noise/Screaming

Birds sometimes make a lot of noise. Some like to scream. This is normal. But it can also be very annoying.

The best way to teach your bird not to scream is to ignore it. Do not look at your bird. Do not talk to her. Walk out of the room if you can. Whatever you do, do not scream back. Your bird will think this is fun and continue to make noise.

Be sure to take a close look at your bird every day. Make sure his eyes are bright and clear. This is a parakeet.

Problems and Challenges

You might also want to teach your bird to whistle or whisper instead of scream. If you reward that behavior with treats, your bird might do it instead.

Feather Plucking

You may notice your bird biting at his feathers. That is part of normal grooming. But if he is pulling out his feathers and biting his skin, it is a problem.

Feather plucking could have different reasons. Your bird may be nervous, stressed, or bored. He might be picking at a wound. There may also be a medical cause.

Your vet can treat your bird for a medical problem. For behavior problems, you must find the cause. For example, if your bird is stressed when you go out, try leaving the TV on. Give him new toys and treats. Get him used to your leaving for short periods and then increase them.

Problems and Challenges

If you do not know the cause, you can try to discourage feather plucking. Mist your bird with water. Bathing will get your bird to do some normal grooming behaviors.

Also, make sure your bird receives enough sleep. You can cover his cage with a dark blue or black blanket for at least twelve hours every night. That could help reduce stress.

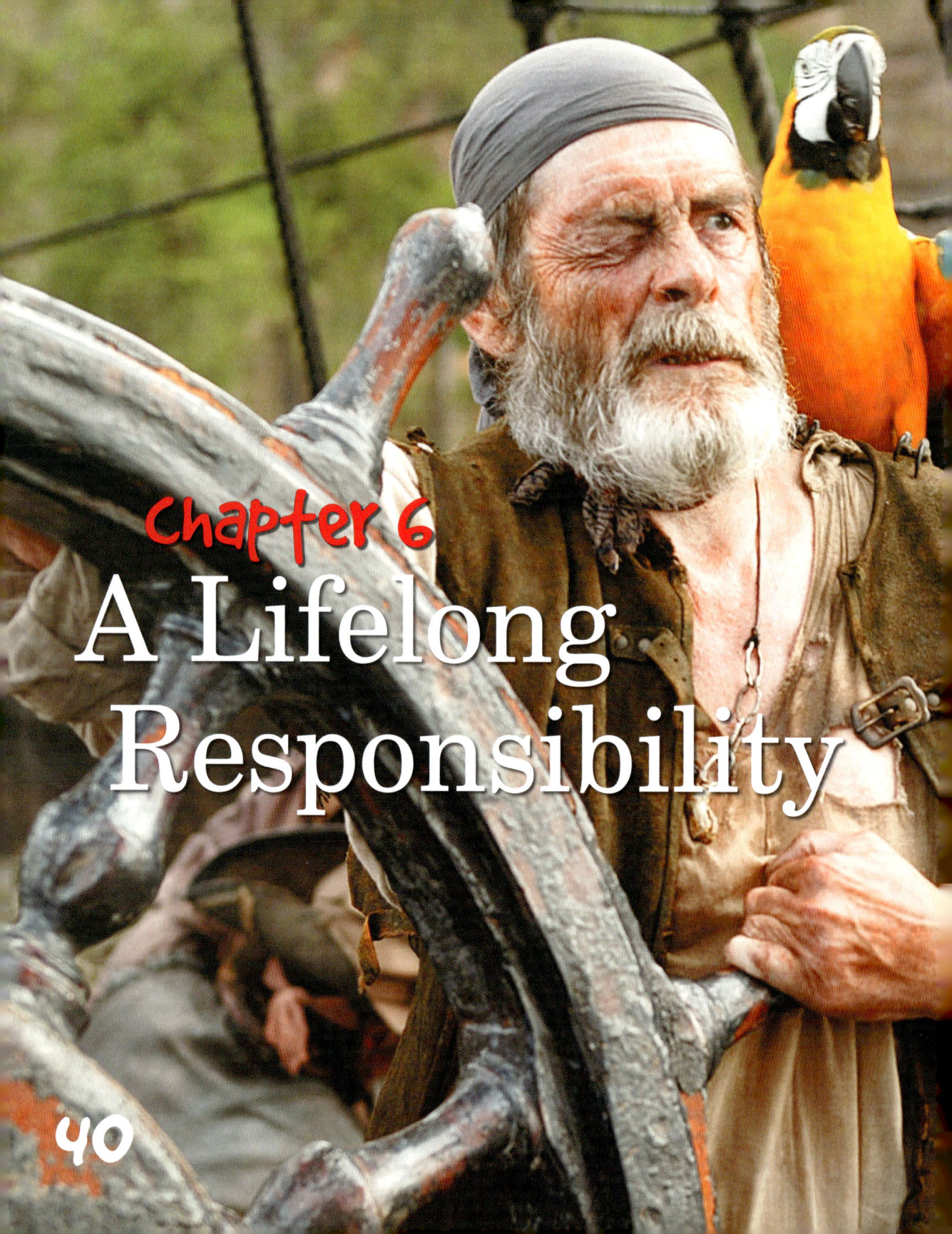

Chapter 6
A Lifelong Responsibility

Birds are in the movies! That's a parrot sitting on that pirate's shoulder in the movie *Pirates of the Caribbean: At World's End*.

In *Pirates of the Caribbean*, you may have noticed a parrot or two. They also appeared in *Peter Pan*. These smart birds can be trained to act a certain way in a scene. They sometimes even have starring roles. In the original movie *Doctor Doolittle*, it is Polynesia the parrot who teaches the doctor to talk to the animals.

A Lifelong Responsibility

Birds make great pets!

When birds appear in the movies or on TV, people get excited. They think about bird ownership. Adults and kids want to own a bird and teach her tricks.

Sharing your life with a bird is very rewarding. But becoming a bird owner is a lifelong commitment. Birds live a long time. The smaller parrots live twenty to fifty years. Larger birds can live even longer. That means your bird might know you as a child and as an adult. She may even know your children. It is not a decision to make until you are ready for this type of responsibility.

Of course, there are many reasons to own a bird. In return for food, shelter, and medical care, birds will give us so much.

A Lifelong Responsibility

Birds can improve our mood. They can keep us from feeling lonely. They are always there to happily greet us. They are beautiful to look at. They squawk and sometimes talk to us. Birds can even be good listeners. In these ways, they reduce stress. They help to make us happier people.

Simply spend the time to care for your bird. Make a difference in his life and you will have a friend for many years.

This is a cockatiel.

Glossary

anesthesia—A special medicine that puts a person or animal into a sleep state so he does not feel pain.

animal shelter—An organization that cares for homeless pets.

commitment—A promise to do something.

mating season—The time of year when birds look for others of their species so that they can produce young.

microchip—A computer chip ID that is placed under the skin of a bird, usually in the chest.

mimic—To copy an action or sound.

molt—To shed a body covering like feathers.

socialize—To get your bird used to people.

species—A specific type of bird that came from a common ancestor.

temperament—Personality.

wingspan—The distance between the tips of a bird's wings when they are held up to the side.

Further Reading

Books

Burnie, David. *Bird*. New York: DK Children, 2008.

Phillips, Meredith. *Bird World*. Mankato, Minn.: Compass Point Books, 2005.

Preszler, June. *Caring for Your Bird*. Mankato, Minn.: Capstone Press, 2008.

Further Reading

Internet Addresses

American Humane Association
   <http://www.americanhumane.org>

Animal Planet—Pets
   <http://animal.discovery.com/pet-planet/>

Bird Watching for Kids
   <http://www.biglearning.com/
   treasurebirds.htm>

Index

A
aggression, 34–35
Alexander the Great, 10
Aristotle, 10

B
bird-proofing (pet proofing), 33–34

C
cage, 15, 21–22
canaries, 11–12, 15
cockatoos, 15, 16
Columbus, Christopher, 11

E
Egypt, 9, 10
exercise, 25, 27

F
feather plucking, 38–39
finches, 14, 15
food, 22–23

G
Greeks and Romans, 10
grooming, 23–25

H
hand feeding, 19

M
macaws, 4, 16
messenger birds, 10
microchip, 27

N
noise, 36

P
parrots, 14, 15
pecking, 34–35

S
sickness, 22, 28
socialization, 30

T
talking birds, 4-8, 10, 30
temperament, 14
types of birds, 14–15

V
veterinary care, 19

48